——— *The* ———

LITTLE BOOK OF

COCKTAILS

Rufus Cavendish

summersdale

THE LITTLE BOOK OF COCKTAILS

Copyright © Summersdale Publishers Ltd, 2014

Research by Sophie Martin

Summersdale Publishers Ltd
46 West Street
Chichester
West Sussex
PO19 1RP
UK

www.summersdale.com

Printed and bound in the Czech Republic

ISBN: 978-1-84953-585-4

Disclaimer
The publisher urges care and caution in the pursuit of any of the activities represented in this book. This book is intended for use by adults only.

Substantial discounts on bulk quantities of Summersdale books are available to corporations, professional associations and other organisations. For details contact Nicky Douglas by telephone: +44 (0) 1243 756902, fax: +44 (0) 1243 786300 or email: nicky@summersdale.com.

CONTENTS

The
ESSENTIALS

THE EQUIPMENT

Cocktail shaker

There are a number of different shakers on the market, including the French style (below, left), Boston shaker (below, middle) and Cobbler (below, right). The favourite among bartenders is usually the Boston shaker.

Bar spoon

A metal spoon with a long, often twisted, shaft.
Money-saving alternative: chopsticks.

Jigger

A two-sided shot measurer.
Money-saving alternative: measuring jug or egg cup, depending on the quantity of alcohol.

Muddler

A stirring rod, usually metal, with a ridged circular end used for crushing solid ingredients.
Money-saving alternative: wooden spoon or pestle.

Fine strainer

An item similar to an everyday kitchen sieve, only smaller and with finer holes.
Money-saving alternative: tea strainer.

Ice bucket (if you're hosting a big party)

A metal bucket, preferably with an insulated structure, that is big enough to hold your required cocktail equipment, such as glasses and ingredients.
Money-saving alternative: anything from saucepans to a small paddling pool (the possibilities are endless)!

Lemon and lime squeezer

Available in the classic glass or plastic version, or the no-expense-spared Philippe Starck Juicy Salif.
Money-saving alternative: your hands.

THE TECHNIQUES

Muddle

This is the action of crushing various ingredients, such as sugar, soft fruits, citrus fruits or mint, to allow flavours to infuse. Press down the muddler in a grinding motion to break up the ingredients.

Strain

This technique helps to sieve out any excess solids, such as sugar and pips, from cocktails to produce a smoother texture. For best results use a fine strainer.

Shake

A common technique used to mix ingredients. Place ice into your shaker with the requisite cocktail recipe ingredients, tighten the lid and apply all your effort into the shaking motion. When condensation has formed on the outside of the shaker and it becomes ice cold, then you know that the cocktail is ready to be decanted into a glass for serving.

Stir

Some cocktails suffer from being shaken because the process forms bubbles that can detract from the appearance and texture of the cocktail. Use a bar spoon to stir ingredients, in steady circular motions. This technique usually means it takes longer for all the ingredients to mix properly, compared to shaking.

Layer

Use this technique when the recipe requires ingredients to be added in a certain order. For perfect results, ensure that the glass and ingredients are chilled, and the shots are poured over a bar spoon to help the layers separate properly.

TIPS FOR COCKTAIL MAKING

1 Try to use as little mixer as possible in your cocktail, unless otherwise stated. Let the alcohol do the work for you, but always remember to drink responsibly.

2 Put cracked ice in your glass, unless the recipe says otherwise. Crushing to a pulp or leaving the ice cubes whole isn't encouraged; by cracking the ice cubes the optimum surface area is gained. This will make the cocktail's temperature and consistency just right, and will ensure the drink is neither too diluted nor tepid before it is served.

3 Use the correct glass for each cocktail to ensure the correct measurement is given – on each recipe page there is an icon indicating which glass to use.

■ – short   Y – martini   Y – poco grande

▮ – highball   Y – flute   Y – margarita (welled)

4 Chill the glasses you use before serving for the optimum cocktail-drinking experience.

TIPS FOR HOSTING A COCKTAIL PARTY

1 If you can, don't leave organising to the last minute. Try to prepare everything before the day of the party, then you can relax and have fun knowing that everything will run smoothly.

2 A special theme will always get your guests in the mood and the conversation flowing. The obvious choice is black tie. Other more creative ideas are a 1920s event, with gangsters, molls and flappers, or get everyone to come dressed in the colours of their favourite cocktail.

3 Play background music that will match the theme of your party, or just add to the ambience. If you are hosting a traditional cocktail party, create a compilation of jazz music and let the lively beats lend themselves to the bustle of people and buzz of conversation.

4 Surprise your guests with a memento of the evening. There will be craft ideas scattered throughout the book to give you some inspiration.

The

COCKTAILS

The
OLD FASHIONED

BELIEVED TO BE THE FATHER OF A NEW GENERATION OF COCKTAILS, THE OLD FASHIONED WAS FIRST CALLED 'THE WHISKEY COCKTAIL' AND SUPPED IN THE MORNING TO START THE DAY WITH A KICK. TO DISTINGUISH IT FROM THE OTHER COCKTAILS THAT WERE BEING INVENTED, IT HAD ITS NAME CHANGED TO 'OLD FASHIONED': MEANING THE OLD-FASHIONED WAY OF MAKING THEM.

TODAY IT IS SEEN IN THE EYES OF THOSE FEW TOUGH ENOUGH TO ENJOY ITS HEADY CHARACTER AS THE ORIGINAL AND TRENDSETTER OF POTENT DRINKS.

Shake

DIFFICULTY: ♈♈   **GLASS TYPE:** ■

REQUIRED: 1 SUGAR CUBE OR 1/2 TSP OF
CASTER SUGAR, 3 DASHES
OF AROMATIC BITTERS, DASH OF
CARBONATED WATER (OPTIONAL),
60 ML WHISKEY (RYE OR BOURBON)

 Put the sugar into a glass.

 Add the aromatic bitters; if new to this repertoire of flavours stick to Angostura bitters, but if you'd like to be adventurous there are lots of others on the market for you to experiment with.

3 Top up with carbonated water (optional).

4 Muddle the sugar while rotating the glass at an angle, so that the sugar grains and bitters create a lining.

5 Add ice.

6 Finally, pour in the whiskey of your choice.

7 Serve with the old-time charm of a Kentucky gentleman.

The

MARTINI

DESCENDANT OF THE SWEETER MARTINEZ COCKTAIL, THE MARTINI HAS BEEN ADAPTED OVER TIME MORE THAN MOST CLASSIC COCKTAILS, EVEN WHERE THE EMBELLISHMENTS ARE CONCERNED. FOR INSTANCE, INSTEAD OF TOPPING WITH AN OLIVE, THE FIRST MARTINIS WERE SERVED WITH A CHERRY. ONLY SINCE THE POPULARISATION OF THE DRINK IN THE JAMES BOND FILMS HAS THE MARTINI ENJOYED ITS FAMED RELATIONSHIP WITH THE OLIVE. BUT ONE QUESTION STILL REMAINS UP FOR DEBATE: IS IT BEST SHAKEN OR STIRRED?

Shake or Stir

DIFFICULTY: 🍸🍸　　**GLASS TYPE:** 🍸

REQUIRED: 35 ML DRY VERMOUTH, 120 ML GIN,
1 OLIVE OR CHERRY

1 Add ice to the shaker.

2 Pour in the dry vermouth, stir briefly to infuse the flavours and strain, discarding the vermouth if not needed again.

3 Add the gin of your choice; a good quality brand and strength will impact the overall quality of the drink. Connoisseurs recommend it should be around 84-proof (47 per cent).

4 Stir, or shake à la James Bond, until the shaker is cold and strain into the glass.

5 Garnish with an olive, or a cherry if keeping things traditional, and sip with the effortless bravado of a true spy.

THE ONLY AMERICAN INVENTION AS PERFECT AS THE SONNET.

H. L. MENCKEN ON THE MARTINI

The
MANHATTAN

CREATED AND NAMED AFTER THE MOST
SOPHISTICATED BOROUGH IN THE BIG APPLE,
THE MANHATTAN IS SAID TO BE ONE OF
THE MOST HARMONIOUS COCKTAILS FOR
FLAVOURS, ALONGSIDE THE MARTINI. WHEN
PERFECTED, THE SIMULTANEOUS BURST
OF SWEET, SHARP AND BITTER
FLAVOURS OFFERS THE TASTE BUDS A
TANTALISING EXPERIENCE.

FROM A PURIST'S POINT OF VIEW THIS
COCKTAIL IS BEST STIRRED IN ORDER
TO PRODUCE A WELL-BLENDED MIXTURE
WITHOUT DISTURBING THE INGREDIENTS.
IF SHAKEN, YOU'LL SOON KNOW FROM THE
WRATH OF ITS MURKY APPEARANCE.

Stir

DIFFICULTY: ΥΥ   GLASS TYPE: Υ

REQUIRED: 70 ML WHISKEY (RYE OR BOURBON),
35 ML SWEET VERMOUTH, 2-3
DASHES AROMATIC BITTERS,
1 CHERRY OR SMALL SLICE OF
LEMON PEEL

1 Pour the whiskey (rye is recommended but bourbon is fine if preferred), vermouth and bitters into the ice-filled shaker.

2 Stir lightly and carefully, but well. Shaking will make the cocktail cloudy to the eye and oily to the taste.

3 Strain the drink into the glass and garnish with the lemon peel or cherry.

4 Pretend you're sitting at the top of the Empire State Building and imagine the breathtaking views as you indulge in this metropolitan cocktail.

GLOW STICK
BALLOONS

Make

DIFFICULTY: 🖊

REQUIRED: BALLOONS, GLOW STICKS, STRING

1 Just before your party, activate the glow sticks by bending them.

2 Blow up each balloon just over its natural inflated size.

3 While pinching the end of the balloon, take the glow stick and feed it into the balloon so it's fully inside.

4 Tie a knot in the balloon.

5 Arrange the balloons nicely and dim the lights when your guests arrive, so that they can admire the iridescent colours.

The

DAIQUIRI

CUBA IS THE HOME OF RUM AND SO IT ISN'T SURPRISING THAT IT WAS HERE THE DAIQUIRI WAS INVENTED. ITS PURE FLAVOURS HAVE STRUCK A CHORD WITH MANY AND IT EVEN GOT A MENTION IN F. SCOTT FITZGERALD'S BOOK *THIS SIDE OF PARADISE*. BUT ITS LITERARY CONNECTIONS DON'T STOP THERE. ERNEST HEMINGWAY HAD A GREAT AFFINITY WITH THE COCKTAILLE ; SO MUCH SO THAT IN ONE SITTING HE POLISHED OFF NO LESS THAN SIXTEEN!

Shake and Stir

DIFFICULTY: ♼

GLASS TYPE: ♼

REQUIRED: 70 ML WHITE RUM, 1/2 TSP CASTER SUGAR, 1 LIME

1 Cut the lime in half and squeeze the juice into the ice-filled shaker.

2 Stir in the sugar and then add the rum. If you prefer to use dark rum, make sure that you don't use as much sugar.

3 Give the concoction a vigorous shake and strain into the glass.

4 Top off your Cuban air with a Havana cigar, whether it's used for smoking or simply as a prop.

The
MARGARITA

THE MARGARITA WAS THE FIRST COCKTAIL MADE WITH TEQUILA AS ITS MAIN ALCOHOL-BASED COMPONENT – A DARING MOVE THAT HAILED FROM MEXICO, THE LAND OF SPICY FOOD AND POTENT DRINK. INCLUDED ON ALL RESPECTABLE COCKTAIL MENUS, PEOPLE HAVE EVEN REWARDED ITS FLAVOURSOME POTENCY BY HAVING A NATIONAL MARGARITA DAY, CELEBRATED ACROSS AMERICA ON 22 FEBRUARY.

Shake

DIFFICULTY: Y Y   **GLASS TYPE:** Y

REQUIRED: 35 ML TEQUILA, 20 ML TRIPLE SEC,
20 ML FRESH LIME JUICE, FLAKED
SALT, LIME WEDGE

1 Using your finger, circle the rim of the glass with
lime juice and put it face down onto a layer of salt,
leaving it long enough so the salt sticks.

2 Pour the tequila, triple sec and lime juice into a
shaker filled with ice.

3 Shake well and strain into a glass.

4 Place a lime wedge on the rim of the glass. Salud!

The
SIDECAR

THE SIDECAR. A COCKTAIL OF TWO CITIES. IT IS SAID TO HAVE BEEN INVENTED SHORTLY AFTER WORLD WAR ONE, ALTHOUGH IT IS UNCLEAR AS TO THE EXACT WHEREABOUTS OF ITS BIRTH. ON ONE SIDE OF THE CHANNEL THE BELIEF IS THAT IT ORIGINATED IN PARIS, *FAIT AVEC AMOUR*; BRITONS, HOWEVER, CLAIM THAT IT WAS A TRENDY BAR IN LONDON THAT FIRST OPENED THE PUBLIC'S EYES TO THIS CONCOCTION.

BOTH WERE INFLUENTIAL CITIES OF THEIR TIME, SO THE COCKTAIL'S VIBRANT COLOUR AND TASTE COULD BE A REFLECTION OF EITHER. BUT NEVER MIND ITS AMBIGUOUS BEGINNINGS BECAUSE ONCE YOU HAVE HAD A TASTE YOU'LL BE GRATEFUL FOR ITS INVENTION, WHICHEVER CITY IT WAS IN.

Shake

DIFFICULTY: ⟁

GLASS TYPE: ⟁

REQUIRED: 30 ML TRIPLE SEC, 60 ML COGNAC, 30 ML FRESH LEMON JUICE, SMALL SLICE OF ORANGE PEEL

1 Combine the triple sec, cognac and lemon juice in a shaker filled with ice and shake vigorously.

2 Strain into a glass.

3 Squeeze and slide the outside of the slice of orange peel around the rim of the glass to transfer its zest and then place it into the drink.

4 Serve with the hospitality of the British and the *je ne sais quoi* of the French.

The

COSMOPOLITAN

FIRST CREATED IN 1970s AMERICA, THE COSMOPOLITAN IS NOW REGARDED AS THE EPITOME OF STYLE AND SASS AMONGST ICONIC CELEBRITIES SUCH AS MADONNA, WHILST CHARACTERS LIKE CARRIE BRADSHAW IN *SEX AND THE CITY* PARADE THE PARTY SCENES WITH THE PINK STUFF IN HAND.

THIS SIMPLE YET TASTY BEVERAGE HAS REMAINED HIGH ON THE COCKTAIL MENU SINCE ITS BIRTH OVER FORTY YEARS AGO. WITH NEW VARIATIONS BEING CREATED ALL THE TIME IT CAN EVEN BE ENJOYED IN THE MORNING, WITH COFFEE-FLAVOURED VODKA, OR IMBIBED WHEN RELAXING UNDER THE PALM TREES IF YOU SWITCH THE VODKA FOR RUM, WITH THE BARBADOS COSMOPOLITAN.

Shake

DIFFICULTY: ▼ ▼ ▼ GLASS TYPE: ▼

REQUIRED: 40 ML VODKA CITRON, 20 ML ORANGE LIQUEUR, 20 ML CRANBERRY JUICE, 1 LIME, SMALL SLICE OF ORANGE PEEL

1 Combine the vodka citron, orange liqueur, cranberry juice in the ice-filled shaker.

2 Cut the lime in half and squeeze the juice into the mix.

3 Shake vigorously until blended.

4 Strain into a glass.

5 Heat the slice of orange peel with a flame until juice appears and place it in the cocktail to add a zesty kick.

6 Garnish with sass and serve with sex appeal.

HERE'S TO ALCOHOL, THE ROSE-COLOURED

OF LIFE.

F. SCOTT FITZGERALD,
THE BEAUTIFUL AND DAMNED

DISCO BALL
COCKTAIL STICK

Make

DIFFICULTY: ✎ ✎ ✎

REQUIRED: TOOTHPICK, PING-PONG BALL, 10-MM-SQUARE MIRROR MOSAIC TILES, GLUE, METAL SKEWER

1 Pierce the ping-pong ball – very carefully! – using the skewer to make a toothpick-sized hole.

2 Glue each tile onto the ball without covering the hole, and leave to dry.

3 Once dry, fit the ball onto the end of the toothpick and fix with glue to secure properly. Leave for several hours to dry.

4 Serve with a cosmopolitan and go back to the disco days when the cocktail made its big appearance.

The

FRENCH 75

THE WORLD WAR ONE PILOT WHO WAS
ALLEGEDLY THE CREATOR OF THE FRENCH 75
COMPARED THE COCKTAIL'S STRENGTH TO
BEING SHOT BY A FRENCH 75-MM HOWITZER
ARTILLERY PIECE, HENCE ITS NAME. HIS
GOAL WAS TO TURN CHAMPAGNE INTO A
DRINK WITH A BIT MORE KICK AND IT SEEMS
HE NOT ONLY ACHIEVED HIS AIM,
BUT SURPASSED IT.

DO YOU THINK YOU COULD HANDLE IT? TAKE
A COMFORTABLE SITTING POSITION AND
SUBMIT YOURSELF TO THE FORCE OF THE
FRENCH 75.

Shake

DIFFICULTY: Y Y   **GLASS TYPE:** ❦

REQUIRED: 35 ML GIN, 8 ML SIMPLE SYRUP
(ONE PART WATER AND ONE PART
SUGAR), 15 ML FRESH LEMON JUICE,
CHAMPAGNE (OR ANY WHITE
SPARKLING WINE), LEMON TWIST

1 Mix the gin, syrup and lemon juice in the shaker,
add ice and shake.

2 Strain into a glass.

3 Top up the rest of the glass with champagne, or
sparkling wine, which is just as good but a much
cheaper alternative.

4 Garnish with the lemon twist, rubbing the excess
juice around the rim.

5 Protect yourself in the event of it blowing your
roof off.

The

BLOODY MARY

A HANGOVER REMEDY IN ITS OWN RIGHT, THIS COCKTAIL IS LOADED WITH TOMATOES, A GREAT SOURCE OF VITAMIN C AND GLUTATHIONE (A SUBSTANCE THAT FIGHTS AGAINST NASTY TOXINS). HOWEVER, THE AMOUNT OF ALCOHOL REQUIRED FOR THIS RECIPE ALONE IS ENOUGH TO GET YOU GOING.

ITS NAME ALTERNATED BETWEEN RED SNAPPER AND BLOODY MARY IN ITS EARLY EXISTENCE IN THE 1930s. THE REASON BEHIND THIS IS REPORTED THAT BLOODY MARY SOUNDED 'TOO VULGAR' FOR THE KING COLE BAR IN NEW YORK WHERE IT WAS SERVED. NOWADAYS IT IS THE MORE COMMON NAME TO USE. BUT EVIDENCE AS TO WHY ITS NAME CHANGED BACK IS AS CLOUDY AS ITS APPEARANCE.

Shake

DIFFICULTY: Y Y Y Y **GLASS TYPE:** ▌

REQUIRED: 60 ML VODKA, 100 ML TOMATO JUICE, 10 ML FRESH LEMON JUICE, 5-6 DASHES WORCESTERSHIRE SAUCE, COARSE SEA SALT, CHILLI POWDER, 3-4 DASHES TABASCO, 2-3 PINCHES OF BLACK PEPPER, 1 PINCH OF CELERY SALT, A PORTION OF CELERY STICK, LEMON SLICE, CHERRY TOMATO, COCKTAIL STICK

1 Mix one part coarse sea salt and one part chilli powder on a flat surface.

2 Using your finger, circle the rim of the glass with lemon juice and put the glass face down onto the salt and chilli and leave for a few seconds until it sticks to the glass.

3 Add the vodka, tomato juice, lemon juice, Worcestershire sauce, Tabasco, pepper and celery salt to a shaker filled with ice cubes and shake vigorously.

4 Top the glass up with whole ice cubes. The Bloody Mary is usually enjoyed as a daytime drink, so whole ice cubes will keep the cocktail cooler for longer and allow you to take your time drinking.

5 Strain the contents from the shaker into a glass.

6 Skewer the celery stick, lemon slice and cherry tomato onto a cocktail stick and add as the finishing touch, complete for you to enjoy with a well-earned rest.

IF THIS DOG DO YOU BITE,
SOON AS OUT OF
YOUR

TAKE A HAIR OF THE TAIL
IN THE MORNING.

SCOTTISH PROVERB

The

TOM COLLINS

THE TOM COLLINS WAS ONE OF THE FIRST COCKTAILS TO COME ON TO THE PARTY SCENE, INVENTED IN 1820 AND ORIGINALLY ESTABLISHED AS THE JOHNS COCKTAIL. ITS RECIPE HAS ALTERED OVER THE YEARS AND CAN NOW BE ORDERED IN A VARIETY OF FORMS THAT ARE DIFFERENTIATED BY USING ALTERNATIVE FIRST NAMES. THE TWO MOST POPULAR ARE THE TOM COLLINS, WHICH USES GIN, AND THE JOHN COLLINS, WHICH IS MADE WITH WHISKEY. OTHER ALTERNATIVES ARE THE JUAN COLLINS, WITH TEQUILA AS THE SUBSTITUTE, AND THE JACK COLLINS, WHICH CONTAINS APPLE BRANDY.

Shake and Stir

DIFFICULTY: Y

GLASS TYPE: ▮

REQUIRED: 60 ML DRY GIN, 30 ML FRESH LEMON JUICE, 1 TSP CASTER SUGAR, DASH OF CARBONATED WATER, CHERRY, ORANGE TWIST

1 Add the gin, lemon juice and sugar in a shaker filled with ice and shake well.

2 Strain into the glass.

3 Top up with carbonated water and stir.

4 Garnish with the cherry and the orange slice, squeezing the orange first to infuse a zesty flavour.

5 Raise your glass to Tom – or John, Juan or Jack, whichever version you decide to experiment with.

The

QUEEN MOTHER

IN REMEMBRANCE OF THE QUEEN MOTHER AND IN CELEBRATION OF THE HEALTH OF QUEEN ELIZABETH II, RAISE A REGAL GLASS WHEN ENJOYING THIS DRINK. KNOWN TO BE HER FAVOURITE COCKTAIL, IT IS ALSO SAID THAT THE QUEEN MOTHER WAS QUITE PARTIAL TO NOT ONE, BUT TWO, GLASSES BEFORE TUCKING INTO SOME LUNCH. HER PERSONAL LIKING WAS FOR THREE PARTS DUBONNET AND SEVEN PARTS GIN.

SINCE THE QUEEN'S DIAMOND JUBILEE AND OTHER RECENT ROYAL OCCASIONS, THIS COCKTAIL IS SEEING A RISE IN POPULARITY AND IS TRENDING ON MORE AND MORE COCKTAIL MENUS.

Stir

DIFFICULTY:

GLASS TYPE:

REQUIRED: 165 ML GIN, 75 ML DUBONNET, DASH OF TONIC (OPTIONAL), ORANGE OR LEMON TWIST

1 Add some ice to the glass.

2 Pour the gin and Dubonnet over the cubes.

3 If you're not as hardened to this intensity of alcohol as the Queen Mother was, add a dash of tonic.

4 Garnish with a twist of orange or lemon peel.

5 Imbibe in a setting that is fit for a queen.

I THINK THAT I WILL TAKE TWO SMALL

OF DUBONNET AND GIN WITH ME THIS MORNING, IN CASE IT IS NEEDED.

QUEEN ELIZABETH, THE QUEEN MOTHER

CONFETTI
THROWERS

Make

DIFFICULTY: ✎

REQUIRED: PLASTIC TUBES WITH STOPPER, TISSUE PAPER IN VARIOUS COLOURS, SCISSORS OR A CRAFT HOLE-PUNCHER

1 Using the scissors or craft hole-puncher, cut or punch the tissue paper into small squares.

2 Fill the plastic tubes with the tissue paper, ensuring a variety of colours are used for each individual tube.

3 Put the stopper on the tube.

4 Celebrate the success of your party by getting your guests to release the stoppers and throw the confetti into the air to create a room filled with shimmering colours.

The
PINA COLADA

THE FIRST PRINTED REFERENCE TO THE PINA COLADA COCKTAIL WAS FOUND IN A 1906 ISSUE OF THE WASHINGTON POST, DUBBED 'PINA FRIA' (COLD PINEAPPLE) AS IT DIDN'T CONTAIN RUM OR COCONUT MILK.

IT WASN'T UNTIL 1922 THAT WE CAME SLIGHTLY CLOSER TO THE PRESENT-DAY RECIPE WHEN A MAGAZINE ANNOUNCED ITS FIRST APPEARANCE WITH THE ADDITION OF RUM. SUBSEQUENTLY, IN 1937 ANOTHER VARIATION OF THE PINA COLADA WAS RECORDED, THAT THIS TIME REPLACED THE RUM WITH COCONUT MILK. THE ARRIVAL OF A COMBINATION OF ALL THREE INGREDIENTS IN ONE GLASS CAME IN 1954, BUT THE IDENTITY OF THE CREATOR OF THE COCKTAIL IN ITS FINAL FORM CONTINUES TO BE DEBATED TO THIS DAY.

Shake

DIFFICULTY: ❚ ❚   **GLASS TYPE:** ❚

REQUIRED: 50 ML PINEAPPLE JUICE, 45 ML
WHITE RUM, 50 ML COCONUT
CREAM, TWO TRIANGLES OF
PINEAPPLE

1 Mix all the liquid ingredients in a shaker and add
ice.

2 Shake vigorously until a consistent texture.

3 Strain the concoction into the glass, or half a hollowed
out pineapple for the full beach-holiday experience.

4 Make a slit down the middle of both pineapple
chunks and wedge on the rim of the glass.

5 Dig out a deck chair, chill to the sound of some
Caribbean music and savour the tropical flavours
of this classic.

MR. STIGGINS WAS EASILY PREVAILED
ON TO TAKE ANOTHER GLASS OF
THE HOT

RUM AND WATER, AND A SECOND,
AND A THIRD, AND THEN TO REFRESH
HIMSELF WITH A SLIGHT SUPPER,
PREVIOUS TO BEGINNING AGAIN.

CHARLES DICKENS,
THE PICKWICK PAPERS

The
JACK ROSE

LEGEND HAS IT THAT THE JACK ROSE WAS NAMED AFTER AN INFAMOUS SCANDAL IN AMERICA WHEN A LIEUTENANT OF THE NEW YORK CITY POLICE DEPARTMENT WAS FRAMED BY GAMBLER JACK ROSE, OVER THE CASE OF THE MURDER OF HIS RIVAL GAMBLER. ALTHOUGH A FASCINATING TALE TO TELL, THE MORE RATIONAL CONNECTION IS THAT THE MAIN INGREDIENT, APPLEJACK, HAS A ROSY HUE.

A DELECTABLE COMPOSITION FOR THOSE WHO LIKE THE PREMISE OF THE SIDECAR BUT WOULD RATHER NOT SUFFER FROM A HANGOVER.

Shake

DIFFICULTY: ▼   **GLASS TYPE:** ▼

REQUIRED: 75 ML APPLEJACK BRANDY, 30 ML
FRESH LIME JUICE, 14 ML GRENADINE
SYRUP

1 Mix all three ingredients in a shaker filled with ice
and shake well.

2 Strain into a glass and serve with a far-fetched
scandal story of your own that will leave your
cronies in disbelief.

BRETT DID NOT TURN UP, SO... I WENT DOWN TO THE BAR AND HAD A JACK

WITH GEORGE THE BARMAN.

ERNEST HEMINGWAY,
THE SUN ALSO RISES

The

NEGRONI

TRADITIONALLY SERVED AS AN APERITIF, THE NEGRONI HAS MADE A COMEBACK IN RECENT YEARS. TRAVEL TO SAN FRANCISCO AND YOU CAN EVEN GET IT ON TAP AT JASPER'S CORNER TAP & KITCHEN.

THE NEGRONI CAME INTO BEING IN 1919, IN FLORENCE, WHEN COUNT NEGRONI ASKED THE BARTENDER IF HE COULD HAVE HIS USUAL AMERICANO BUT WITH MORE OF A KICK: REPLACING THE SODA WATER WITH GIN. LET'S HOPE THIS TIME THE NEGRONI, AS A MODERN CLASSIC COCKTAIL, IS SET TO STAY.

Stir

DIFFICULTY: ΥΥ   **GLASS TYPE:** ▮

REQUIRED: 35 ML CAMPARI, 35 ML SWEET VERMOUTH, 35 ML GIN, SMALL SLICE OF ORANGE PEEL

1 Pour the ingredients into an ice-filled glass over a bar spoon.

2 Stir until thoroughly mixed.

3 Heat the slice of orange peel with a flame until juice appears and place it in the cocktail to create a zesty kick.

4 Salute!

THE MANHATTAN, THE DRY GIN MARTINI AND THE NEGRONI COULD BE CONSIDERED THE TRIPLE

OF THE COCKTAIL KINGDOM.

GARY REGAN

The

TEQUILA SUNRISE

YOU MAY BE FAMILIAR WITH THE TEQUILA SUNRISE CONTAINING A LARGE AMOUNT OF ORANGE JUICE. ALTHOUGH THIS IS THE MOST POPULAR WAY OF MAKING IT TODAY – A TREND THAT KICKED OFF IN THE 1970s – THE TEQUILA SUNRISE'S DEBUT RECIPE BEARS LITTLE RESEMBLANCE IN TASTE, YET REPRESENTS THE SAME BEAUTIFUL SUNRISE IN APPEARANCE.

TAKE A LEAP OF FAITH AND EXPERIMENT WITH THIS ORIGINAL, SADLY NEGLECTED RECIPE. IF YOU LIKE IT, WHY NOT START A REVIVAL OF THE OLD-SCHOOL STYLE.

Stir

DIFFICULTY: 🍸🍸🍸 **GLASS TYPE:** 🍸

REQUIRED: 50 ML TEQUILA, JUICE OF 1/4 LIME, 20 ML CRÈME DE CASSIS, CARBONATED WATER, ORANGE SLICE, MARASCHINO CHERRY

1. Pour the tequila, then the lime juice, over a bar spoon into a chilled glass.

2. Layer the crème de cassis on top of the other ingredients, again over a bar spoon.

3. Top up with carbonated water.

4. Garnish with an orange slice and a maraschino cherry.

5. Take a moment to admire the spectrum of reds, oranges and yellows, then stir the drink and enjoy the taste.

The

SINGAPORE SLING

AROUND A HUNDRED YEARS AGO, A MAN
NAMED NGIAM TONG BOON WAS SAID TO
HAVE INVENTED THE FIRST SINGAPORE SLING
WHEN HE WAS WORKING IN THE LONG BAR AT
THE RAFFLES HOTEL.

THE VIBRANT COLOUR, REMINISCENT OF
THE WARM COLOURS OF THE SUMMER SUN
SETTING, IS ENOUGH TO TEMPT ANYONE TO
TASTE IT AND WILL CREATE AN EXOTIC
ATMOSPHERE WHEREVER IT IS SERVED.

Shake

DIFFICULTY: Y Y   **GLASS TYPE:** ▮

REQUIRED: 70 ML GIN, 15 ML CHERRY BRANDY,
7 ML GRENADINE, 7 ML D.O.M.
BENEDICTINE, 20 ML ORANGE
JUICE, 15 ML FRESH LIME JUICE, 2
DASHES BITTERS, ORANGE SLICE,
MARASCHINO CHERRY

1 Combine all the ingredients in the shaker, add ice and shake until there is a significant head of foam on the surface of the concoction.

2 Strain the mix into the ice-filled glass.

3 Top off with a slice of orange – cut down the middle and wedged on the rim of the glass – and a cherry.

4 Transform your sitting room into a scene reminiscent of the Long Bar, equipped with blow-up palm trees and white-suited waiters.

PERSONALISED SEQUINNED GLASSES

Make

DIFFICULTY: ✐✐✐✐

REQUIRED: COCKTAIL GLASSES, SEQUINS AND GEMS, WOOD GLUE

1 Buy some cheap cocktail glasses (plastic ones will suffice) and sequins and gems of your choice. A craft store will provide a range of colours and sizes for you to choose from.

2 Before your party, stick the sequins and gems onto the glasses using the wood glue. A thoughtful touch is to personalise each glass with a guest's name, so that at the end of the night no one will forget to take theirs home. And, if you want to get a bit creative, there's plenty of inspiration to be found on the Internet.

3 On your guests' arrival, fill their glasses with a delicious cocktail and let them admire their printed name on the glass.

The

RAMOS GIN FIZZ

LUXURIOUS, SILKY AND IRRESISTIBLY TASTY (THAT'S IF YOU GET IT RIGHT). THE RAMOS GIN FIZZ IS A HARD DRINK TO MASTER BUT THE EFFORT YOU PUT IN IS DEFINITELY WORTHWHILE. A DRAWBACK FOR MANY IS THE INCLUSION OF RAW EGG WHITES, BUT IF YOU CAN STOMACH THEM, GIVE THIS A GO.

TO MAKE THE PERFECT RAMOS GIN FIZZ, THE ORIGINATOR HENRY C. RAMOS AND HIS GANG OF BARTENDERS AGREED THAT THE DRINK MUST BE SHAKEN CONTINUOUSLY FOR 12 MINUTES TO CREATE A PERFECT MERINGUE-LIKE TEXTURE. DON'T WORRY – THIS TRADITIONAL METHOD ISN'T FOLLOWED ANYMORE, UNLESS YOU FANCY WORKING A FITNESS REGIME INTO YOUR COCKTAIL MAKING.

Shake

DIFFICULTY: Y Y Y Y Y **GLASS TYPE:** ▌

REQUIRED: 60 ML GIN, 30 ML DOUBLE CREAM,
1 EGG WHITE, JUICE OF 1/2 LEMON,
JUICE OF 1/2 LIME, 2 TSP SUPERFINE
SUGAR, 2/3 DROPS ORANGE FLOWER
WATER, DASH OF CARBONATED
WATER

1 Add all the ingredients into a shaker filled with plenty of ice.

2 Shake the mixture vigorously for at least two minutes, but if you're feeling resilient try going for the full twelve!

3 Strain into the glass and top with the carbonated water.

4 Enjoy the silky texture and let it send you into a dairy dream, topped with a smattering of tipsiness.

The
WHISKEY SOUR

THE WHISKEY SOUR WAS FIRST OFFICIALLY MENTIONED IN *JERRY THOMAS' BARTENDER'S GUIDE* IN 1862. HOWEVER THERE IS SOME EVIDENCE TO SUGGEST THAT IT BECAME POPULAR AT THE UNIVERSITY OF VIRGINIA, IN THE JEFFERSON LITERARY AND DEBATING SOCIETY, THE OLDEST KNOWN UNIVERSITY SOCIETY, DATING BACK ALMOST TWO CENTURIES. THE YEAR THE WHISKEY SOUR WAS INTRODUCED TO THESE MEETINGS IS UNKNOWN, ALTHOUGH THE FAMOUS GOTHIC AUTHOR EDGAR ALLEN POE WAS A REGULAR PARTICIPANT AT THESE DISCUSSIONS AND IS SAID TO HAVE FAVOURED THE BITTER INFUSION AND POTENCY.

Shake

DIFFICULTY: ΥΥΥΥ **GLASS TYPE:** ■

REQUIRED: 60 ML WHISKEY (RYE, TRADITIONALLY USED, OR BOURBON), 30 ML FRESH LEMON JUICE, 1 TSP CASTER SUGAR, 1/2 EGG WHITE (OPTIONAL), MARASCHINO CHERRY, SLICE OF ORANGE PEEL

1 Dissolve the sugar in the whiskey by stirring in a shaker mixed with ice.

2 Then add the lemon juice and egg white (optional) and shake vigorously. If adding egg white make sure to shake the mixture at least a minute longer in order to create a thick texture.

3 Garnish with an orange peel held over a flame for a couple of seconds and a cherry.

4 Start an incisive discussion with friends while enjoying the drink.

The

MAI TAI

IF YOU DON'T HAVE AN EXCUSE TO DRINK A MAI TAI COCKTAIL FOR THE OTHER 364 DAYS OF THE YEAR, MAKE SURE YOU DO ON 30 AUGUST, HAWAII'S NATIONAL MAI TAI DAY.

ALTHOUGH IT IS UNCERTAIN WHO THE CREATOR WAS, 'TRADER VIC' BERGERON, FOUNDER OF THE TRADER VIC'S RESTAURANT CHAIN, IS KNOWN TO HAVE POPULARISED IT. THE FIRST GUINEA PIGS WERE TWO OF HIS TAHITIAN FRIENDS WHOSE RESPONSE TO THE COCKTAIL WAS *MAITA'I ROA AE*, MEANING 'OUT OF THIS WORLD, THE BEST!' FROM THEN ON THE SHORTENED NAME MAI TAI HAS STUCK AND HAS BECOME THE GLOBAL MONIKER FOR THIS DELICIOUS CONCOCTION.

Shake

DIFFICULTY: ♈ ♈   **GLASS TYPE:** ■

REQUIRED: 35 ML LIGHT RUM, 35 ML DARK
RUM, 35 ML ORANGE CURAÇAO, 17
ML ORGEAT SYRUP, JUICE OF A LIME,
MARASCHINO CHERRY

1 Pour all the ingredients except the dark rum into a
shaker with ice cubes and shake well.

2 Strain into a glass half-full with ice.

3 Add the dark rum into the glass over a bar spoon to
help it spread more evenly.

4 Garnish with the cherry and say 'Mai tai!' when
experiencing its out-of-this-world flavours.

CANDY
IS DANDY
BUT LIQUOR
IS QUICKER

OGDEN NASH

The

PLANTER'S PUNCH

SAID TO HAVE BEEN INVENTED IN THE 1650s, THIS IS BY FAR THE EARLIEST COCKTAIL TO EMERGE, AND LONG BEFORE COCKTAILS BECAME THE IN DRINK AT BARS AND PARTIES. PLANTER'S PUNCH IS COMMONLY THOUGHT TO HAVE ORIGINATED IN JAMAICA, HOWEVER, MORE RECENTLY THERE HAVE BEEN CLAIMS THAT CHARLESTON, AMERICA, IS ITS MOTHERLAND, WHERE IT WAS CREATED IN THE PLANTERS HOTEL.

WHEREVER YOUR IMAGINATION LEADS YOU, BE IT ONTO THE BEACHES OF HAWAII OR TO THE QUAINT STREETS OF CHARLESTON, TAKE ADVANTAGE OF THIS BLEND OF FANTASTIC FLAVOURS AND PRETEND YOU'RE IN PARADISE,

Shake and Stir

DIFFICULTY: ♈ ♈   **GLASS TYPE:** ♉

REQUIRED: 30 ML DARK RUM, 30 ML LIGHT RUM, 15 ML ORANGE CURACAO, 50 ML ORANGE JUICE, 50 ML PINEAPPLE JUICE, 15 ML HONEY, 15 ML WATER, 1 LIME, DASH GRENADINE, DASH BITTERS, SLICE OF ORANGE PEEL, CHERRY

1 Add the first five ingredients to an ice-filled shaker and shake well.

2 Heat the honey and water in a saucepan and stir until a consistent, runny paste.

3 Then add it into the mixture with the juice from the lime, grenadine and bitters and stir well.

4 Strain into a glass, garnish with the orange peel and cherry, and enjoy while tuning your mind to the sound of lilting waves or hum of city life.

JEWELLED
CANVAS BAGS

——— Make ———

DIFFICULTY:

REQUIRED: PLAIN CANVAS BAGS, PENCIL, TEMPLATE OF A COCKTAIL GLASS, SEQUINS AND GEMS, JEWEL GLUE

1 On the canvas bag, stencil around a cut-out of a cocktail glass; there is a cornucopia of templates that you can print out on the Internet.

2 Then apply the sequins and gems using jewel glue onto the bag, filling in the outline of the glass. One effective colour scheme is to use only one colour, but start with a dark shade at the bottom and gradually get lighter.

The

LAST WORD

A COCKTAIL THAT EMERGED IN 1920s AMERICA – IN THE THROES OF PROHIBITION – AND CREATED NOT BY A BARTENDER BUT A STAGE PERFORMER. ALTHOUGH ITS NAME SUGGESTS BOLDNESS, ITS DWINDLING PRESENCE MEANS THAT IT HASN'T MANAGED TO GAIN A POSITION ON THE COCKTAIL MENU FAVOURITES.

TRY IT TODAY, SAVOUR ITS CRISP FLAVOURS AND BE SURE TO SPREAD THE WORD ABOUT THE LAST WORD.

Shake

DIFFICULTY: Y   **GLASS TYPE:** Y

REQUIRED: 35 ML GIN, 35 ML MARASCHINO
LIQUEUR, 35 ML GREEN
CHARTREUSE, 1 LIME

1 Add the first three ingredients into a shaker filled
with ice.

2 Cut the lime in half and squeeze the juice into the
shaker.

3 Shake well and strain into a glass.

4 Serve to your guests with the persona of an
exuberant stage performer to make your cocktail
evening one they will never forget.

If you're interested in finding out more
about our books, find us on Facebook at
SUMMERSDALE PUBLISHERS and follow
us on Twitter at **@SUMMERSDALE.**

WWW.SUMMERSDALE.COM